THE CAT THAT SHAT

THERE ONCE WAS A CAT...

THAT ALWAYS SHAT

HE SHAT ON THIS

HE SHAT ON THAT

HE SHAT ON YOUR BROTHERS
BASEBALL BAT

HE SHAT ON A RAT

HE SHAT ON A MAT

HE SHAT ON THE DESK OF A LAZY BUREAUCRAT

HE SHAT ON A HAT

HE SHAT ON A GNAT

HE SHAT ON A MAN WHILE HE SCREAMED...

WHEREVER HE WENT HE LEFT BEHIND SHAT

HE OFTEN SHAT WHEREVER YOU SAT

HE EVEN SHAT

ON THE TAIL OF A CAT

ONE TIME HE SHAT

ON A JAR OF PORK FAT

USE A TOILET? NO! SAID THE CAT

I'M A LAZY CAT

WHO LIKES TO LAY FLAT

YOUR JOB IS SIMPLE

TO CLEAN UP MY SHAT

BAA BAA BLACK SHEEP
Deals With Another Routine Stop

Only $10

Baa baa black sheep please step out of the car. Yes sir yes sir please know I'm unarmed. Do you know why I stopped you today?. "Because of the fur color I display?". You match the description of a suspect I seek. Funny it's the 4th time to happen this week. I profiled you because you are black. And you drive a Mercedes which seems kinda whack.

Does Anyone Know Whatever Happened To
MURDER HORNETS

Remember Murder Hornets? Whatever happened to them? We dive deeply into the terror phenomenon that never came to be. 2020 had so many bigger things, so Murder Hornets were forgotten.

Make Your Own Luck

What can pimps and divorce lawyers teach children, about money and luck? This book tells the story of outdated wisdom and harsh truths.

Cockroach-baby smells really musky. Centipede baby was sewn from human skin. Squid-fish lives deep down in the sea. Flesh-eating ladybug is super scary. Bearded baby was born this hairy.

CREEPY CREATURES
KEEPING YOU AWAKE WITH QUESTIONS

STICKERS

Do you like...
CHEESE

OURS BABY
The Only Child Your Step Mom Loves

Your stepmom wants one thing from your dear old dad. Viable sperm and an empty house. Pack your bags it's time to grow up.

MOMMY GOT A DUI

Your mom has secrets. She hides her drinking from you… Until now. Mommy can't drive you to school and you're going to have to learn the bus routes.

INSOMNIAC & FRIENDS
The Clowns That Put You To Sleep

Yeetyeet likes to watch you sleep. Pickles under your bed he creeps. Switchblade eats your favorite stuffies. Pedo lures you away with puppies. Shifty plans to collect your teeth. Twisty smells your hair while you sleep. Clammy lives inside his van. Hank once had to kill a man. Tooty smells your dirty socks. Busby laughs at electric shocks. Twinkles spends the night robbing graves. Fappy keeps a few human slaves.

MY RACIST GRAN

WHY DADDY HITS MOMMY

A Kids Guide To Understanding Alcoholism

TRIGGERED
Kids Guide To Cancel Culture

Easily offended is the new trend. People act outraged. Be careful, you might lose your job. Even though nobody is responsible for the feelings of others.

OK BOOMER

Boomer always complains at the store. But it was on sale yesterday!! When yesterday's special isn't available anymore. You shouldn't be such a slut. Boomer gives unsolicited advice. This smart phone is dumber than dirt. Boomer always struggles with his device. Boomer demands your supervisor.

CINNAMON

A horse forced into the sex trade.

Only $10

DON'T BATHE WITH UNCLE JOE
Setting Boundaries With Adults

Uncle Joe lost his job. For misconduct in the workplace. He's coming to stay with us. You're going to have to learn to avoid his hands and more importantly. NEVER bathe with uncle Joe.

Only $10

THIRST TRAPS

Why Moms Phone Keeps Blowing Up

DADDY'S A SIMP

Don't Expect Much Inheritance

YOUTUBE.COM/C/BRADGOSSE

BRADSY.COM

TIKTOK.COM/@BRADGOSSE

BRADGOSSE.REDBUBBLE.COM

AMAZON.COM/AUTHOR/BRADGOSSE

INSTAGRAM.COM/BRADGOSSE

FACEBOOK.COM/THEBRADGOSSE

TWITTER.COM/BRADGOSSE

Brad Gosse

Printed in Great Britain
by Amazon